Peter Waine is a former chairman of the Campaign to Protect Rural England, of the Tree Council and of the National Fruit Collection at Brogdale. He is author or co-author of a book on the countryside, a collection of poetry, two business books and a novel. He has been on main boards of both public and private companies and is a former trustee of the Royal Opera House and visiting professor at both Warwick and Cass Business Schools. He was a judge in 2017 and 2018 for the Wainwright Prize, celebrating the best in nature writing.

To Kate

And thank you again

for all the splendid work

you do for the Centenary!

Litri

Peter Waine

2020

'To the highways and byways that content me.'

Peter Waine

AS I GO A WANDERING

A love letter to the English countryside

With paintings and poetry by the author

When you return to Digswell and I am long since gone

AUSTIN MACAULEY PUBLISHERS™

LONDON • CAMBRIDGE • NEW YORK • SHARJAH

A CIP catalogue record for this title is available from the British Library.

ISBN 9781528921466 (Paperback)
ISBN 9781528922180 (ePub e-book)

www.austinmacauley.com

First Published (2020)
Austin Macauley Publishers Ltd
25 Canada Square
Canary Wharf
London
E14 5LQ

Author's Note

This manuscript is a love letter to the countryside enhanced by poetry I have written and pictures I have painted and underpinned by a deep affection for the countryside gleaned from a lifetime associated with it and often helping to protect it.

Introduction

We are indeed fortunate in this country to have on our very doorsteps incomparable countryside, the result of nature and human activity with a liberal and enviable historical ingredient peppered throughout.

In my case, queens and prime ministers, Roman generals and incalculable unknown men and women add interest and reason to stand and stare, to pause and reflect on our island story, all within a few miles of my home.

And this little piece of England is not unique, not by any means.

We need the iconic landscapes that are dear to us, but we cannot rely upon them on a regular basis. For most of us, they are faraway places.

So, to go out and explore what is around the corner, is a solution and a meaningful answer. There is simply so much to enjoy and a slight variation, cutting across a field rather than heading for the usual sty, can give a totally different feel to an otherwise familiar walk. And it is free, all free thanks to those who campaigned to protect our green and pleasant land; they had vision and we are their beneficiaries.

Do not leave it for another time. Each season is special and if we are ignorant of what is there or complacent, then we might lose it to a needless or thoughtless development. Gone, gone forever.

Summer green the verdant hills.
Beyond the ridge then furrow all for me to see
And free!
What joy, what bliss
Where and how compare?
I know not, neither do I care.

Oh the joy when I turn off the lane, up the bridle path, along the old way, passing glades, accompanied by glimpses of open fields and distant views, then I cut through, meander along the path beside the hedge to join the larger track and, turning right, I enter the inner gates of arcadia.

At heaven's gate both thrush and blackbird sing
Whilst waxing moon will wander through the night
The roosting bat will take to wing
The night unfolds.

Yet there are few who even know these ways, however long they have lived in these parts and yet, again, it is no more than seven miles from the nearest underground station—in fact, a mere 12,320 yards.

The views are endless, the variety of vistas numberless and they change constantly, each day and with the seasons.

I walk the fields and byways
My spirit strangely free.

I pass the hedge where, in late summer, the blackberries grow, offering their fruits free and in abundance. There I steal a moment in the darkening day, alone but happy. There is a late and distant sun.

The brambles have recently shed their white flowers, little observed, unspectacular petals; they carpet the ground, the first embrace of autumn, a sign that summer, despite the skylarks above and the waving corn, has passed its peak.

So soon the summer fruits
Foretell the passing year.

No matter. Each season has its delights even if some hide their beauty more successfully than others. Spring and summer, especially spring and in England, that long unfurling and unfolding act of expectant delight. Ostentatious times, like youth but unlike youth which passes, and never to be renewed, the rising sap of the countryside returns. Hard to believe at times of dank darkness when the lanes are dripping, the nights are long and silence pervades, interrupted only by the splash of boots on the soggy earth, the deepest, wettest spots— always the same ones—sometimes impassable, frequently a challenge.

The rutted field in winter
Is filled with water now.

In summer, the rutted lane, made so by walkers and compounded by tractors, becomes baked and indented, adding atmosphere to the walk. A branch will fall and walkers make a detour. Fine except when thereby bluebells are compacted into oblivion.

Bluebells chime where only Heaven can hear.

***

I pass the same walker today as I passed yesterday and at the same place. The dog welcomes me again and the owner ignores me again. I say hello, perhaps too quietly, but surely, we are kindred wayfarers or is he a reluctant walker taken out by his dog?

Next two horses, their riders thank me for standing aside. Astride these beasts, the rider can see at an advantage, higher with panoramic views and without the disadvantage of being detected by the nostrils of nature.

I can map their route by the fresh droppings. Nothing wrong with that. Some droppings are almost pleasant, that of horses as they plod or gallop down the lanes being one, whilst that left by the careless dog walker is quite another matter.

The house is now in view or rather the railings and the hedging, the grand paths and the stone column, the orchards and the fountains, the lions on their pillars, the distant gables, and the pavilion for the pool nearer to hand.

The lane here, as it passes between the laurels on the field side and the railings and plantations on the other, reminds me of Victorian and Edwardian pictures, the ones I looked at with my grandmother who introduced me to nature and to plants in particular. I often wonder, when I do this walk, whether she would have recognised the link. Probably not.

It comes and goes forgotten,
the laurel's white caked flower,
Unlike the bluebell where the woodland once had been
It never has its hour.

The house is a delight. It adds meaning to the surroundings. History and nature combine, an intoxicating mixture which an old, old country like ours can convey. When I leave the proximity of the estate and cut down through the verges—ignoring the frequent 'Private Keep Out' signs, the owner has 27 acres to himself—I looked it up—I can enjoy the views of his woods almost as much as can he!

And the view through the woods is wonderful. The bracken at this point in high summer is as tall as me—the growth of a single season and supplemented by the rays of sunlight under a cloudless sky, to become brown and broken at the year's end.

The bracken brown in autumn rain
Where soon as shelter wren will find
A welcome home from winter's days.
Whilst on the bank, beside the ways
A woodland spread of narrow fronds
Yellow or green, upright or down
And brambles hide the woodcock well
Where gusty winds old branches fell.

***

There are furrows, high banks, reminiscent of the ones in the woods above my beloved Dunster. Are they like the latter, ancient boundary markers, or of a more recent origin with a mundane meaning?

The path is almost sandy here and it leads me to the set aside, today a cacophony of wild flowers and accompanying butterflies as wonderful, in its different way, as a Gertrude Jekyll herbaceous border. And like a well-planned border, the flowers of the meadow, of the hedgerow, of the field margins have an array of colour and of hues which always complement and never clash. The blue of the chicory, the lilac of thistle, the yellow of ragwort and of tansy, the white and yellow oxeye daisies, with the white of spring blossom on the hedgerow

13

and the red berries of the autumn, with the pinkish-purple of the wild teasel bordered by its prickly surround, making a brief entry in high summer when the skylark is above and, at noon, there is a stillness in the air. The brush of nature makes complete. (I make a note to steal a few oxeyed daisies in late autumn that are out in the field just before the plough finishes them off. I have an ideal spot for them in my wild garden.)

However, I view it all with mixed feelings; is this a brief respite, to be ploughed next year? I draw some solace; at least it has been a haven for wildlife for the last three or more springs and summers and maybe, just maybe, this little patch can remain without depriving people of second homes or second helpings of food.

> *When splash of red is mixed with heaven's gold*
> *And lark ascends the patchwork view*
> *In mellow fields the poppies stand*
> *Before the silent dusk descends*
> *The skylark reigns supreme.*

It means cutting through the overgrown terrain to re-join the main path at the lip of the hill, but well worth it. When there the views are spectacular, 'spectacular' to me who has loved them in all seasons but who stops to stare, to wonder. The countryside allows me to think, to dream.

> *The heart will home my secrets all*
> *One more as days are new*
> *And sighs to hold my heart at bay*
> *The many turned to few.*

The lanes they share my secrets
Each walk a line or two
A pause for sad reflection
On this and that and you.

At this point, to the left, are wooden protective surrounds for the young oaks. In winter, they take on a more sinister mantle; they could be gibbets, the backdrop for a doomed Hardy or Housman lad passing on his way.

Later, the lane hugs a spinney with a dip in the middle, very shear banks, the trees in the bottom reaching the ground level of the top with their canopies. Maybe an old working, now no doubt a special habitat.

High banked the path that leads to nowhere now.

Further on before the turning right to reach the gorse and the same estate, are the pine trees. They whisper to each other in the summer breeze and chatter like old friends in the winter storms. About here, a summer or two ago, I passed someone I knew from the village green. We chatted. She and her friend were walking across the fields to a pub, which by road was a reasonable distance, but by foot, direct, was much shorter. She said she kept her front door key in her bra. I said hitherto I wondered what bras were for; we laughed, they moved on and within a short time, when I turned, because we were walking in different directions, they were surprisingly far away.

The path back has a character all of its own but how can that be when to my right are the woods, the fields, the trees, which I passed only a moment before? At a junction, I turn left up the grassy set aside, with skipper butterflies zigzagging in front of me as if to check the terrain and escort me. They are busy butterflies and today they are out in numbers. I feel guilty because one of them persists in flying in front of me but it could have deviated to the left or right as did its cousins, its uncles and its aunts. So we are both at fault, blame apportioned equally.

Where in winter stolen walks are made
On grassy banks and meadow fields
Butterflies in vibrant blue display
And rabbits play
Pure joy.

There is another sign warning me to keep out. This time it is on a shorter stake and I can almost claim in defence and mitigation that I didn't see it. At the top the path cuts across the field of corn, earlier a soggy track to be renewed following ploughing; now a recognised route again, to the green way and back to the beginning—with one little delight before the final turn. In the field beside the path, near to a hedge, can be seen in winter, albeit faintly, the evidence of a building. Something once stood where the soil is disturbed, now lost in harvest time and ignored or overlooked in winter. It was once and is no more—like me.

Others will transgress—trespass—these ways when I am gone, forgotten, a footnote of another season.

Thatched and lichened clad, the stone barn stands
Amidst the ripening corn.
And where a stone has gone, the tit resides.

* * *

Close to my house is a lane, I have a copy of a map dated 1599 with the lane exactly as it is today with fields, woods, open space and a house. Nothing added or subtracted. How many folk in previous times must have plodded that way? Men with their sons, the sons with their children, the mothers and sisters doing their daily rounds. All gone, all forgotten, yet once they were here, as I am. Today is my day, but like them, I have no tomorrow. So be it. And on the open road news would have arrived of the Black Death with its pending consequences, news of victory at Trafalgar, of world war, of the blessings of peace. All that adds to the natural scene, to its intimacy, to its relevance, even to its enrichment.

In the field beside the lane, the ponies munch away their day. Sometimes, in the hottest periods, I wonder what they are finding to eat and if I pass them at night, with the owls hooting in the dark sky and with the foxes and the muntjacs barking, the ponies continue to munch away.

The noises of the night, the darkest places do not phase them so nor will they me.

As I return home, I glance at the rowan, which I planted many years ago and which is now a fine established specimen. It is a worthy addition; I haven't seen a witch since its planting—none before for that matter—but there are, I am sure, more fairies than hitherto.

***

A walk which I do frequently accumulates a rich and poignant collection of memories and associations, even if, in time, they will inevitably merge into one. I pass the gate to the yard where I last saw Anne, a true Christian who led the Sunday group and needed her faith to sustain her during her divorce and terminal illness which took her away all too soon. I last saw her here, we chatted and she cried. It was our farewells, yet the only topic not discussed was precisely that. There was no need. We both knew. She was moving away, having to, and I never saw her again.

The fork here in the lanes could be an ancient junction, cut out over the decades, consolidated down the centuries, as carts cut left, then right, or went straight on, and then from the other direction creating a small haven for wildlife which holds out today.

I wish I was familiar with the field names and no doubt I could be, if I really wanted to. They add meaning to a landscape, an ingredient unique to an old country, even when the names might be repeated in countless other hamlets. Names like moat piece, fishponds, kennels, warren piece, a glimpse of the past, reflective of heavy toil. Of course, the names meant less than the quality of the soil and its location, of the climate and of its husbandry.

***

I know my hedges and I know they often marked an ancient boundary between two lords at war.

Dull skylark gives the sweetest song
Sound of heaven than earth belong
With age the hedgerow takes its name
And choicest show of fare to claim
Where feasting eyes should linger long.

To see them as a patchwork stretching far into the distant horizon, a sense of practical order, is a huge delight. One hedge, beyond the ridge after passing through a plantation and a spinney or two from the Palladium church, is home to a dozen or more sparrows, always there, peculiar to that spot, to be found nowhere else in these parts—a little quirky idiosyncrasy of nature. Recently I walked Bredon Hill in summertime, as Housman said, but possibly never did, and saw the fields and patchwork of hedgerow and the barrows, ramparts, the villages, the glimpse of the abbey and barn, the great stranded whale of a hump of the Malverns and the hint of distant Wales, so different.

The hedgerow in its glory now
From lowly dip to distant brow.
Four quarter moons the poppies bloom
By bridle path and dreamlike comb.

Many can read a hedge by looking at the variety of species in its midst.

The hedge its moment comes again
With autumn mists and closing days
And berries red on naked twigs
As spindle leaves show pinker fair
With thorns against the greying skies
Stands long beside the bridleways.

For me it is sufficient to know where the cornflowers grow; I like to visit them and thank them when nobody is looking or overhearing for just being there, being cornflowers and not being some exotic thing introduced or escaped. Some will say, grandly, that plant X was introduced purposefully—perhaps by the Romans for good measure—and that on occasion we should be suitably grateful. Escaped from number 42 more likely—they left their gate open—an alien to all.

***

Not all boundaries around here are delineated in this way. We have a river which once divided Saxon England from the Danes and a stone beside the cricket boundary, which determined the boundary—long disputed—between the Abbots of St Albans and of Westminster. How about that! Kingdoms delineated and a place where two great medieval abbeys disputed their shaky claimed inheritance. Oh, I almost forgot; the said boundary stone, despite its significance and longevity, was moved a few feet to allow the cricket boundary to be marked more fairly. No wonder the land hereabouts is called Nomansland. Most driving past, as I risk my life crossing, wouldn't know all this, nor I guess and fear, in many instances, even care.

The rays of sun play through the webs of time

Such is life and with a generation brought up on a different fare. When I walked the Icknield Way from my daughter's village to find the tumuli, and when I think I found them, appearing as yet another manmade hump of very recent origin, on the golf course, asking a golfer in the adjacent rough whether I had indeed found this ancient leftover, he said he didn't know and implied he didn't care. To believe that a tumuli is of less importance than a round of golf is evidence of a deep malaise.

***

I try and make amends when next in church for my momentary intolerance. Our church, an arts and craft little brick masterpiece, is the third—the other two around the corner from the location of the present one, with only an overgrown churchyard, the last resting place of soldiers from the Punjab and of long living and long serving rectors, to remind us of their former location.

In the silence of the night
I heard Christ weeping
For his fractured world
Or did I dream whilst sleeping?

But then the rays of sunrise
Break the ice-cold dawn
Robins raise their young
Stubborn hope engulfs the morn.

* * *

I once helped clear the old churchyard, replacing a stone slab to keep the spirits in and to encourage a more diverse habitat. It was fun and hard work, but I knew that within weeks the brambles would return, like the incoming evening tide, and our efforts would have been of merely transitory usefulness.

In church today, a small congregation and I wonder whether we will remain open. Bless the Lord that we will!

The dove upon the steeple
Will give our peace a say.

Two new faces to me—one turns out to be the daughter of a farmer who farmed here 60 years ago, a prospect of an earlier rural economy. She worked in our house when it was a corporate headquarters for a brief period in its long existence. The other was the daughter of a former rector whose mother had recently died, but well beyond her three score years and ten.

When oxen ploughed the western weald
And snow lay in the parson's wake
And lark and owl did mark the hour
And honeysuckle paint the tower
Then Eden's gate was opened wide
And I did live before I died.

We were told not to sing the starred verses, no doubt because they were politically incorrect. I always read those first and then ponder especially the last verse of the *Te Deum*, blessedly still central to our litany. '*Oh Lord, in thee have I trusted; let me never be confounded.*' I want that as my epitaph.

I visit the churchyard to see the graves of those who attended faithfully and especially of those I knew but who are now resting in perpetual neverness, with gravestones weathering and looking as if they were resting for more centuries than the few years since their passing. We planted poppies in the margins in memory of the First World War but they haven't taken.

A splash of spring the canvas now conveys
By hedge and ditch and open fen displays
Beyond the poppied splendour tucked away
Wild rose, primrose, bell flower, wild mint and hay.
And rippled moss by crystal moving stream
Compounds, sustains the spirit's wildest dream.
The swifts return with summer in their wake
Their agile turns displayed by land and lake.
By deepest hush the welcome dusk descends
A chapter starts, another chapter ends.

We also planted a yew from a cutting from a tree alive at the time of the birth of Christ and that is flourishing and will, hopefully, be there at the conclusion of the next millennium—a living, continuous link.

I helped develop the concept of a millennium maze with these special young yews, to be planted as a maze on the meridian line and full of symbolism—12 apostles, 12 months of the year, 12 signs of the zodiac, based on the maze in Chartres Cathedral. But it never happened. Another story.

From vigil through to compline stand
The patient yew does clutch the hour
Whilst rusted plough the furrowed land
And resting suns will grace the tower.

* * *

In late spring, the supreme displays of bluebells adorn many of our local woods both around the church and also further afield, along the lane as it dips and turns towards the open views, often enhanced with dapple shades and looking resplendent. So much of that display is centred on our countryside; the woodland floor is touched with blue. We are indeed blessed.

Bluebells grow where woodland once had been.

They are one of nature's greatest colonisers, with every piece of the woodland floor covered and they are clever with their timing, completing their annual cycle before the canopy unfurls, and light is scarce.

* * *

One favourite walk takes me past a wood of bluebells beside the field where once stood a mighty stately pile, where there was once a lake and where a former prime minister fished and landed his catch. The great house has gone, the lake is now a field or two with only the graceful stone bridge to indicate to the casual walker of what was there before. Further along the woodland edge, tucked away, are the remains of the nineteenth century water pump but long since silent and retired, resting, until, no doubt, it too crumbles away.

That walk is a mini delight, taking me over the bridge, along a path which divides the bluebell wood from these other fields, passing a seat where possibly nobody ever sits.

Let me sit and contemplate the view.

Then across another field, where in spring the hares will box, to a corner gate and then left over the top—a bit grand but the feeling is so—and down the minor road to a lodge. And where nearby on one occasion I picked up a stone and found that it was a fossil of a sea sponge. So waters once covered these tranquil acres. Nothing seems permanent and what is here now will no doubt change one day beyond recognition.

The earth grows old
Yet young again by season's new
Then bell by toll the steeple far
Will call the hare to break of day
And insects drone on summer hills
Each one by one the story told
Oh, endless days yet cruelly few.

The skylarks sing above and the view to my left, especially, is uplifting with familiar sights acting as markers a little further south to remind me of another grouping of my favourite walks. Two different worlds but only a field or two apart.

And the lark in flight ascending.

***

Over the years, our adjacent woods, mainly of hornbeam, have been managed with feeling and professionalism, but not without controversy with the removal of evasive rhododendrons. In their place the heather has spread and what a display when the sun draws out its full, glorious pink and purple against the Scots pines and the denser woodland surround. It spreads so quickly, re-establishing ancient terrain.

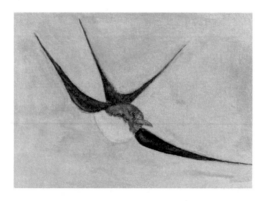

The heather pink and purple now
On vacant moor and open heath
Whilst harebells toll their fairy bells
On slender poles.
And bees will sap the nectar fair
And swifts below an evening sky
Will twist as black then turn as bronze
On days like these.

I learned today that swallows and swifts are not related, that one merely adapted the appearance and habit of the other. I had to sit down on hearing that. What else do I seemingly know but don't, observe but do not see?

***

How easy it is to vary the character of a walk merely by making a small detour and following it, however closely, to the original, as I did due to forced circumstances when, armed with my new binoculars, I detected a small herd of bullocks blocking the gate across the field.

I make a detour left and enter a wood before opening to a field with a cherished set aside decorated by butterflies in profusion. The path beside the field leads through high growing crops and then gently descends the lane. Today, on my right is a small pile of feathers; a pigeon did not make the dawn like its coo which is never completed.

***

I am no recluse but solitude is a necessity. We are a noisy species and few are the places not effected by either light or noise pollution or by both and with pylons marching naked unceremoniously across the landscape, often marring the most prominent views.

> *The lane is long and narrow*
> *Then wide through pastures green.*

There is a spot off the original route which has an abundance of holly and the holly has a great abundance of berries—one of my secret supplies to deck the hall at Christmas—but I never do. At least the equivalent supplies of blackberries are raided—a harvest gathered in by me.

> *The hedge of holly, ash and cherry fare*
> *Portray the foxglove, swallow-herb*
> *The hedgerow and the lanes combine*
> *For lovers' time as those before*
> *Harbours long the primrose flower.*

Amongst the cluster of walks—in that other place over the rim of the undulating hillside—is a particular favourite because it can be added to, joined and enjoyed in a variety of ways. And along the way is another wood which I swear is carpeted by wild daffodils.

> *A lovely sight the willow,*
> *The oak is lovelier still*
> *The secret in the hollow*
> *Is the wild daffodil*

Yes, I am more certain as I glimpse beyond the immediate wood.

> *The daffodils are dying*
> *Their heads are hanging low*
> *Speedwell in profusion*
> *Break forth and overflow.*

Further still is a phoenix tree. I am bragging; I know such trees when I hardly know the difference between a cedar of Lebanon and a cherry tree. The phoenix was an old favourite, two branches growing upwards from the fallen trunk as if they were separate trees, as one day they will become—or one will, the other has fallen since I last passed this way. As I turn, I am sure the tree in front is a black mulberry, perhaps a clue that this was once a parkland. On the turn I am welcomed by the Shetland ponies, or by a few, with most continuing to munch or ignore me. Lovable in appearance if not necessarily always in character.

At the end of this field I turn left up the lime tree avenue where George Bernard Shaw would walk from his house to visit friends nearby. The avenue is a time capsule; fashionable especially in the eighteenth and nineteenth centuries.

The lime tree avenue I walk today is a little lopsided in appearance. On one side, the owner has allowed the side shoots to proliferate and form huge balls like carbuncles, but on the other, where briefly a new golf course was laid out, it is all cut back. Where the golfers played, Galloway cattle graze and plod wearily over the bunkers, which appear now like great ant hills or ancient tumuli.

When I pass the estate that once belonged to George Bernard Shaw via another lane and peer at his writing hut at the end of his garden and think that he wrote so much there and that his ashes are scattered hereabouts, I stop and ponder but it has no effect on me. I wish in a way that it did. However, to pause and ponder and to acknowledge and to visualise the youthful Lawrence of Arabia bounding up the garden, with a draft of his masterpiece the Seven Pillars of Wisdom, under his arm, a far cry from the legend bedecked in flowing Arab robes. Now that affects me.

I like to smell and admire the dog rose here and it prompts me to undertake another walk before long which has a better display.

Wild rose, dog rose, briefly hold their sway
White petals, pink and yellow, short their day
A week or two then wind will blow away.

They might be common but they are native. They didn't escape even from Shaw's garden. The roses here are a darker pink than those on the other walks but they have a chance here to climb to the heavens, spreading their floral display over the top of the trees like an exploding firework, in sweet scented clusters.

Did I see your loveliness in that rose at dawn?

Houses, locations, the surrounding countryside, all changing but constant reminders of a glorious or interesting past. Within a few miles of home was once home to three queens of England, one a sovereign, two were consorts— and of three prime ministers and two Tudor/Jacobean equivalents.

The lonely lane defines the fields,
As clouds above the sky.

The lane which takes me up from the field where I cross from the Palladium church, passes the back of Katherine Parr's home where Henry VIII courted her and adjacent to a house where an exiled king took refuge in a foreign land during the Second World War. The former cannot have changed much in 500 years; it has an ancient air, a timeless aura, genuine, incredible and all in mint condition thanks to the success and enthusiasm of the present owner.

***

Another walk takes me past the church where the Queen Mother's ancestors rest and where she was baptised near the house where she was possibly born. There is a memorial to her in the churchyard, a sort of modern market cross, beautiful in its appropriateness and fresh in its simple execution with her crown depicted on top—I pause when the sun catches the crown and the weather vane beyond—and the recording of the various titles she enjoyed during her long life—Duchess of York, Queen etc.—but no reference to her ever being Empress of India. I enquire to be told that the Foreign Office deemed it would be politically incorrect. More likely, surely, the titles merely refer to the titles by which she was best known at different periods in her long life. At the beginning of the lane from the house to the church, a lane the young queen must have walked, I once saw a kingfisher, only once, years ago, but it is imprinted on my mind, opposite a quaint gothic styled cottage near a temple and the long, sweeping avenues which are a feature here.

Beyond the church and as the lane opens up to a view of the estate cottage, with its stag horns adorning an out building, I am the recipient of two treats. In the field to the right there is a large herd of fallow deer, watching me, scattering, pausing and disappearing. Closer to the cottage, there is a rainbow, low arched and there but briefly.

***

I am angry. Just returned from a walk, in fine fettle, who wouldn't be passing the ford still surprisingly high considering the long dry summer—where does all the water come from as there are no mountains nearby nor even noteworthy hills, and where wavelets foam its pebbled shore.

Up the lane, passing the estate cottages on my left with their pleasant symmetry and distinctive design, complemented by the painted dark old fashioned green of this particular estate, looking forward with quiet reassurance and mounting expectations to glance at the view to my right, where in the distance Bunyan preached—I find the evil deposits of fly tipping!

Alas, it has been a frequent occurrence in these parts and this spot has proved to be a particular favourite despite the warning signs, the owl notices, apparently watching but clearly not deterring. Hitherto, I was against capital punishment.

I recover thanks to the proximity of nature and to the reassurance that the council will clear away this selfish mess, to find another pile at the bottom of a gentle incline. Again, another common spot for these evil folk.

At the top of the lane is a pond, or rather a dry patch where once there was one. It is one of the first to exit with the arrival of full summer and the transformation of spawn to frogs needs all the evolutionary dexterity in order to complete the cycle in time. Alas, a few do not make it, evidence their squashed remains on the lane. I have little time to ponder their fate; a van, a large van, attempts to squeeze past, no doubt taking a short cut or being told to take this previously idyllic rural route by its satnav. At least mine says "please" when it tells me to do such selfish, crass things and no doubt I pay a hidden extra for the privilege.

At the next turn, but just in the field and indeed at the top of another walk, are three round rotting bales. Why abandoned and why there? Gently over the last couple of years, for that is roughly how long they have languished, grasses are colonising, gradually disguising and metamorphosing them back to nature. Meanwhile, it is probably an ecological gem.

* * *

Today with the hot weather and being July, the butterflies are a cloud of colour, profusion and busy. They are a great show, no need to shout encore as they oblige without being asked—and will continue, no doubt, long after I have walked on. One floats skywards, like a mini kite against the endless blue and cloudless sky. Thankfully, whilst we might produce fly tippers we have advanced in another respect; we no longer collect the butterflies, nor think weirdly that to kill one will bring us good luck. The heath fritillaries, the faithful large white, beautiful today against the many coloured flowers—and my faithful skippers—were all there to entertain me. Of course, I know they do it despite my largely unwelcomed presence—like flowers that bloom in my garden not for my personal edification and pleasure although they give that and in abundance—but as part of an evolved evolutionary cycle of raw survival.

Some species seem to be able to accommodate and accept more willingly our intrusive and dominant nature. Sometimes no doubt it is the result of being unfamiliar with humans and therefore we hold no calculated threat or with familiarity are not perceived as a peril. I noticed this recently when walking in central Scotland; I could almost step around or through the busy gathering of birds on the track. They were blissfully unconcerned.

This happened also and more surprisingly, being a mere seven miles from the nearest underground and in our supposed overcrowded island, on my walk when I crossed an open field where in winter I saw coming through the engulfing icy fog, two walkers, ghostlike, who, as they passed, whirling dense fog engulfed them and they were gone. But this time there was a pair of yellowhammers. The loveliest of birds, little gems, the culmination of creation, indeed its song was the reputed inspiration for the incomparable Beethoven.

How can anyone, therefore, (but they did in ancient days) associate these little wonders with the devil! I tried to share my enthusiasm for what I had seen, but nobody seemed more than politely interested. I suppose you have to see them, experience them, in order to inculcate that rich emotional flow of appreciation for such a bird.

And all the way home on that walk I was accompanied, high on the wing and floating on the wind, just below the hint of clouds, by a buzzard, soaring, watching, complementing the rolling fields below.

The yellowhammers' unexpected display was on a par with the one afforded last summer by dragonflies resting on the rocks beside the Palladium bridge.

And dragonflies in tones of red
Or orange wings and patterned green
Land on path and fence and water's edge
Or sunny ledge
True joy.

***

One is never quite certain what delight is in store when starting each walk; that is part of its inherent attraction. I am sure, despite the utter improbability, that I discovered a new species of either moth or butterfly on a walk I completed recently. The said species appeared again a few days later in a neighbouring vicinity. It was of small/medium size, mainly a divine red but with a strong, distinctive grey marking, like a streak or spearhead from the mid top of its wings to about a third of the way down. Or again the time I saw an exotic little number flitting around the base of our fountain. It was an escaped Australian finch, rather tame but, alas, unlikely to survive the coming winter or the unwelcome attention of native species. I took a picture of my moth/butterfly but only with its wings closed.

Some escaped species, of course, do survive, establish a foothold and colonise—or remain viable in a locality. One such example in these parts are the wallabies in the woods a few miles from my pattern of walks. I have never seen them but then nor have I seen the Loch Ness Monster yet "believe".

Confirmation of their existence—the wallabies not Nessie—came again recently when walking the green way. I spoke to a rider who said that he had often seen them being so high on his horse, nature neither seeing nor detecting his presence, his smell or movement.

I returned via the new ditch, the latest attempt, of many, to avoid winter flooding only to be welcomed by my resident robin, a bird with the best PR around, voted our favourite and depicted everywhere, yet in reality a bit of a bully.

Each note more perfect than the last
How can that be
Yet true I know
The robin on my apple tree.

One of the least heralded marvels of high summer are the thistles—I love it when they readily colonise the set aside even if their tenure will be brief. They come in so many varieties and their flowers, on closer inspection, are truly a work of art, a perfect composition and a lovely colour, with some, such as the cotton thistle, rising mightily beside my path, often exceeding six feet, the growth of a single summer. And in the early morning light they put on a special display.

The spider spins and at first light
The thistle in its webbed delight.

Like other species, the thistle can help me read the land, interpret the landscape through where I walk. I can know how the land has been used, disturbed, ignored or abandoned.

A week no more
Before the thistle blooms
And I to heaven be.
Ignored, passed by
Cut down and scorned
Yet all to me

My own favourite, the meadow thistle, is the most instructive of all. When it appears, I know I have entered an old hay field—few, alas, in these parts, but in the confined, secret corners of a forgotten field, they grow and I draw the nectar of their simple beauty—and get inspired by their determination to survive.

It is ungrateful of me to forget so easily and quickly the different displays of nature but understandable whilst inexcusable because there are so many players, so many acts and no intervals.

As catkins paint the parting day
And bid the winter months away
While silver shade on sallow trees
And purple mist on northern breeze
With yellow hints on hazel trees
A perfect day to me.
And next to wait but not for long
The cuckoo's long departed song.
Then homeward thoughts of tea.

* * *

When the cow parsley paints its way across swathes of verges, almost joining up the sides of a damp or silent lane, the spirit soars. They are a blessing too for our little church at a time when flowers are in short supply and Lent is over and when we like to decorate with representative species from the adjacent lanes. I like its folk name, one of many that this trusty companion enjoys—fairy lace—but cow parsley it is to most of us. Few can compare to their mantling of the lanes with fairy lace.

Fragrance of the evening calling,
Heavy with the scent of love.

On one walk, through and beside the newly planted acres of our largest new woodland, albeit linking patches of ancient forest, I was met with a blanket of oxeye daises, acres of them, swathes of them, introduced but soon to settle naturally into this newly created habitat even if they will not offer an equal display every year as other species arrive and the woodland changes and matures. Perhaps some of the seeds were dormant and were awakened by the plantation, as poppies can do after decades of forced but patient sleep.

Just taken a call on a walk—never a wise thing. After all, a principal reason for such ventures, for me at least, is to accommodate the pressures of modern life, to be refreshed naturally and to put all into some order and perspective. It was to say that I was runner-up for the chair role of the largest grouping of conservation bodies in the world. Oh well. I said they had made the right choice, that the winner was a worthy one.

Why so generous? I wanted that one. Partly, perhaps, because he was the better candidate but also because looking down, I saw the welcome nods of a cornflower and beyond some dog rose, the latter a more subtle combination of colours than I had ever seen before. And then a glance across the field to see the dying—or maturing—harvest of broad beans. The year has turned and so, probably, has my life. Too old, too male—too right!

> How many summers still to see
> And larks to hear ascending
> Or blossom pink upon the tree?
> These are the thoughts and dear to me.

That view is typical; to the naked eye a combination of natural wonders stretching undisturbed and as far as the eye can see, yet through my binoculars there would be a number, probably many buildings dotted around or in clusters in the distance announcing a village or the outskirts of a town.

If I had won half the positions I was runner-up for, my mortal remains would be—at the insistence of a grateful nation—deposited with much fanfare in a vault in Westminster Abbey instead of where they will go, between the church tower and the wall of the priory gardens, set in a West Country National Park, an intimacy for eternity. Thank God.

This lane today is a symbol of defiance; along the edge, despite its width, the council in their insensitivity, and despite my pestering, have cut back the edges. There is no rhyme or reason for snuffing out a season, and spring—and spring in England at that! Yet, despite the council's wasteful expensive endeavour some hedge bindweed—a pink variety—is blooming. Not my favourite but it is present here either because it grew back quickly or because it kept its head down whilst the cutters did their bit and best. With nothing to climb they remained perhaps at ground level and survived to bloom another day.

***

Some plants are touched by folklore and romance, their old-fashioned or alternative names, a link with a rural past. There are so many names. Let me name a few. We have the fairy lace but also cuckoo's stocking, whinny luck, ranting widow, Granny's sour grass, Cat nut, Mary-spilt-the-milk, weasel-stout, rat's tail, Our Lady's candle, travelling sailor.

I think we have the gist. Oh, and how about Tod-tails, floppy dock, Eye of the Child Jesus, Claggy Maggies. Stop! Just one more—Venus's basin. And I will leave it to others to look up their familiar names for in so doing they might discover a treasure trove of endless wonders many to be found on their proverbial doorstep, or passed hitherto unnoticed further afield.

* * *

I am somewhat perplexed. Passing the steep escarpment, possibly one of the last vestiges of the long Chilterns, ever since I have meandered these parts, there has been a statue of the Goddess Diana, albeit a one-legged version, in the woodland, looking down to the river. Now it has gone.

How can a one-legged Diana achieve that, unless it has collapsed and become engulfed by the vegetation, or, more sinister, stolen? But who would want to steal a one-legged Diana? A two-legged one maybe, but not this one.

The walk later takes me past the stud along which the mallow grows—common by name but not so in these parts, a mauve variation rather than the more usual common pink. Romans surely went this way as there are two Roman villas nearby and the supposed site of a mighty battle between Caesar and Cassivellaunus is also a mere few fields away. To imagine that a Roman bent down to eat this plant, so many generations back, believing that it held medicinal qualities making him fitter possibly to march involuntarily to die in a battle and for a cause he didn't understand or care about.

This walk is a convenient one, long enough for refreshment and reflection but near enough to commence on foot from home and to complete when time is at a premium. One part, below where Diana once hunted with her good leg, the path widens and has been gravelled by the council, at a time when there are potholes on the highways and few traverse these parts.

Fortunately, the verges are already converging and the hardy, plucky weeds, are colonising the vacant middle where few walkers seem to tread. It creates a pleasant compromise; the gravel hardly urbanising or intruding, unlike the pylons in the distance or the noise of traffic far away. But then I have already touched on that.

* * *

It is important, indeed imperative, to seize the hour, for soon by evening calling as the poet might say. Hours soon become the full score of our mortal time and each season has its own delights but they are often too brief.

The field beside my drive is covered with meadow buttercups like a bespoke and well-fitted carpet and how that flower ever got the name Devil's guts, is beyond my comprehension. My local buttercup field is cut when in its full display and ethereal prime, when it touches the senses and makes its statement. Then the field falls silent, becoming routine, a small single piece of the jigsaw, one of many, but briefly like childhood, it was there.

Buttercups surely are a masterpiece of nature's engineering, almost surpassing anything due to "a rare combination of structural and pigmentary colouration" revealed by "miscrospectrophotometry and anatomical dissection."

The tales of England told.

When I pause to look at their depiction in a church window, not an uncommon choice of subject in times past, I wonder what happened to those who were young and played with me, when buttercups were merely colourful accompaniments.

* * *

When I walk on the Icknield Way, where Romans and Saxons did long before me, and follow the path as it drops down into the mini valley, to the fold where stands the church on its terraced ridge, beyond the field deformed by old ant hills and now grazed by cattle, I am in for a surprise.

Not just a lane to me
But a footpath to eternity.

33

The hamlet it serves is smaller than it was in the nineteenth century and its congregation probably smaller still, but I am making a little pilgrimage to a church which has a window which retains, and this is almost a miracle, some medieval stained glass portraying the birds of the meadow and surroundings as it was all those summers ago, including lapwings. Few, alas, are to be seen here today.

To my right is the stone surround of a window removed from the local leper colony, almost biblical in its remote connotations and now incorporated sleepily in a timeless way into a forgotten corner of this modest house of God. Outside the wildflowers in their seasons keep loyal company with the silent incumbents of the churchyard and will do so for eternity.

In time the newly dug grave, lovingly well attended, will become less so as those who once knew the dead themselves meet the grim reaper, their preordained destiny, and then the stone, weathered and almost forgotten will be removed and propped against the wall. But the wildflowers will keep their seasons and mark the hours.

One recent grave had a fluffy toy which says it all; the grave of a child—and for added poignancy, it was beside a person who had exceeded his three score years and ten and by a great margin. There is nothing in all the world, or on my walks at least, so sad as a child's grave with its cuddly toy and as I return, I see the toy weather and quietly disintegrate.

The Icknield Way is not one of my regular walks. The previous time was when the spring was late, when winter lingered long and the ground was especially wet.

Spring on hold, the cherry faintly pink.

How can this be the same place and so soon afterwards? What a variable wonder, this stage management of nature, the prop department of creation, ever busy, versatile and ready for a surprise performance.

The final section of the walk takes me along a track but this part gives me little pleasure. It is a necessity, merely a link between the start and the walk itself, yet pretty in its way, rural for all that. But it doesn't have the right feel, not for me at least. Can a lane, a track, have a chemistry and appeal to some and not to others, like people can and do?

They are cutting the grass in the fields today, the hay wafting its scent into the clear summer air. Intoxicating, incomparable. Do the grasshoppers, ever present companions on this walk, hop out of the way in time either because they detect the cutters or because of some innate knowledge inculcated, passed down from one generation to the next? I look out across the plain from this ridge.

Softly tread the distant view.

I am melancholy today. Why? A silly reason but personal to me. The iron railings, so common around my school when I was a child, are also common here, bent, unmaintained but here. It reminds me of a girl. We were only each aged seven and she will have soon and long forgotten me. But the fence brings it all back, leaping like one of those grasshoppers through the years, making passing time meaningless, without its sting. And it must have been beside her that I sat on a hard floor and heard a talk on birds.

The speaker came to the school. He only had what today would be regarded laughably as basic pictures, rudimentary visual aids, of birds on charts but he engaged with me. I haven't forgotten the occasion even if he, no doubt, had by the next day. We never know how or when or to what degree we might influence someone, especially the impressionable young, an open eager book, hopefully for the better. I must try and remember that more often.

**

There are few gates around here because there is relatively little livestock but gates have a rural language all of their own, both practical and emotional.

> *The kissing gate so aptly named*
> *When last I came this way*
> *My luck was then to not foresee*
> *In hopeless love, so helpless me.*
>
> *It was a time of greatest joy*
> *Youth and spring combining*
> *But now the gate is broken down*
> *And I am old and pining.*

The bramble closes off the path
As time has quenched my joy
The gate now leads to emptiness
And time, my love destroy.

When I visit a village pub to cut my thirst, there are often a plethora of agricultural implements hanging from the ceiling or hugging the walls, evidence of hard labour as country folk of earlier eras toiled in order to glean their barely adequate sustenance. But I am suspicious; there are simply too many hay forks and the like. Someone must be making them to order or else country folk were inordinate hoarders.

***

Our church is beside the fields with only three other buildings in the vicinity. At harvest festival time we can sometimes hear the tractor ploughing.

The fields are tilled to wait the summer air.

The representative produce is deposited on the alter steps and the foliage fills and decorates in profusion every available stone sill as the autumn sun lights the final moments of a dying day, through dusty stained glass to the glory of God— and in memory of those who prayed here or served before.

The distant rays of sunshine
Portray the parting view
The fields give way to ploughing
Before spring winds renew.

We are blessed; we can celebrate harvest without reverting to the supermarket shelves, three of God's bounty for the price of two. Ours is a link with the soil, a simple reminder and an easier reason to be grateful.

***

The walk beyond the location where the big house and large lake no longer exists offers an additional attraction today. There is a mighty structure of hay, hardly a haystack, more like a hay skyscraper, large blocks to the heavens reminiscent of a dusty depiction of the Tower of Babel. In previous summers more modest versions would, on occasion, be left to rot and I couldn't understand why. Today, however, the tractor, one man, one machine with forks like a pallet collector, wedging effortlessly between each great block, is lifting them tirelessly, turning, taking them away, one by one, for storage elsewhere. In times past the rural army of local land workers, of all ages, whole families, their animals included, would have undertaken what is today a routine task, replenishing their strength and fortifying their souls with a pint of ale at the King's Head or, more appropriately, at the Hole in the Wall. A four-day job that today takes an hour or so and hardly a calorie expended or a bead of sweat on the brow.

To church. Asked at the last moment to read the lesson. Being a reading from the New Testament I assumed, foolishly as it turned out, that mine was the second reading. A pause, the rector begins his walk to the lectern. I realise then that I should be there and so make a hasty leap into place. Full of apologies afterwards but with ample Christian forgiveness from the churchwarden and from the rector—the latter in a line going back to the twelfth century—I take refuge in the churchyard.

God's Acre. So much heartfelt interpretation and even in a modest location like ours. No doubt some of the plants here will have originated from posies, others from flowers placed in mourning on a child's grave—rosemary for remembrance perhaps or forget-me-nots.

Who will note my passing when I'm gone
Or mourn me as the losing of a friend
Will you note my absence with a sigh
Or will the lamentations be pretend?

For sure, I know of one who will be true
The curious wren in dextrous flight
Inclement weather, sunshine, light or dark
Equal friendship and to each delight.

Some churchyards might be the last refuge for living things such as meadow saxifrage or even of green winged orchids.

One passing thought on the young millennium yew in our churchyard and looking to the future rather than reflecting on the present or on the passing of a child before it has a past—that yew will sustain birds with its sticky berries and maybe the birds will spread the seed as jays do with acorns and thereby establish a mighty oak through their digestive system and dextrous flight. Ah the jay—a favourite of mine. They frequent my garden, noisy, jaunty in flight, hardly a nightingale in song, but that blue feather more than compensates. They are to me the clarion cry of the countryside.

By tossing reeds and alder swamps
I heard the bitten boom
Before the gentle autumn tint
When leaves will boast their rustic glint
At close of day
The doughty jay
Conveys the acorn home.

Whilst we were unsuccessful in establishing poppies in our churchyard to commemorate the centenary of the conclusion of the First World War, outside the confines of God's Acre and with no assistance from churchwardens or anyone else, are the wood anemones known to some by their much more endearing name of Grandmother's Nightcap. Like a beloved favourite grandmother, they seem to have been there forever and, indeed, they are a sure indication of ancient woodland. Their progress is tortuously slow, like the advance of the Allied troops in that war, some say a mere six feet in a century— and so six feet since the silencing of the guns on the western front. In spring, they bring hope of revival.

Today the churchyard is silent, appropriately so as the stillness accompanies the eternal rest of its incumbents. Further down the lane soon after turning right to walk between hedge and field is the beginning of the long abandoned concrete posts for the wire which acted as the fencing for what was once a railway line and now a fine elevated walkway, built, no doubt, by hand and in use for a mere century at most. But the posts are a recent, and in some ways, welcome addition to the archaeological interpretation of this little piece of rural England, more genuine by far than the "Roman" pillar protruding from behind the hedging of the great house at the end of a fine walkway before it stops abruptly at the field's edge. Probably a moulded version but again it looks the part and one day, if it stays *in situ* long enough, it too will become a reference point of this little rural corner.

The field edge is covered in one spot by clover, evidence perhaps of frequent footfall or more likely the remnant of a sown crop.

I listened to the fortune teller
All that I was told
I never found my four-leaf clover
Nor my pot of gold.

Yet not long ago, with one of my grandchildren and whilst chatting about the four-leaf variety and its relative rarity, which I confessed I had never seen despite looking for over 50 years, she exclaimed that there was one beside her foot! She didn't understand its rarity. There it was in all its modest yet deeply symbolic glory. To her it was as common as a daisy but I insisted that it be pressed and it survives to this day.

On my return, I pass a few cottage gardens, always a lovely interpretation of all things floral and old fashioned. Perhaps a bit of borage here and broad bean there, maybe a foxglove or two over there, a wild geranium near the path and is that fennel beyond—and look at the honeysuckle beside the tap!

And honeysuckle binds two hearts as one.

If I look closely, I might find wild strawberries—but no sweet peas! Such gardens are a haven, an easy reference point for simple effortless contemplation. Walk past a cottage garden with its chaotic proliferation and overhanging array of old varieties of this and that, with glimpses of another small section always just beyond, maybe an old pump or a seat, or a view of a corner of the cottage itself, and all confined by definition to a small space.

The Canterbury Bells are out by June
But the columbine is out by May.

These cottage gardens are a bit different; they are feet away from a cutting of a motorway, from a hard shoulder, from the constant passing of cars, coming from nowhere, going somewhere. The contrast, the Kate Greenaway garden and the modern artery to commercial gain, is a strange juxtaposition, a little confusing.

Back on the main road, before crossing to take the path home, I see a notice advertising an event. Not too intrusive and a blessed change from the unremitting, in your face, array of these commercial things that our Continental cousins inflict upon themselves and what we did until stopped by successful campaigning by my beloved CPRE in the 1920s.

But even this local sign is unwelcome because it is still there despite advertising an event which finished over two months ago. Surely the person responsible for putting it up would remember also to take it down as too should others who very likely would have been local or on the organising committee.

It is a little disconcerting; suddenly unexpectedly and continuously for the last couple of days every time I go down the drive, I have a grey pony which insists on attempting and, alas, always succeeding, to stare me out. To begin with a pleasant little distraction but now a psychological torment. Why should a previously placid object on which I have bestowed the friendliest of gestures become thus possessed, beats me.

* * *

Today I was reminded that as with the best designed gardens, the best views are also in compartments, separate rooms making it impossible to see or appreciate the whole in one single glance. Having just re-emerged from the path which takes a direct route through the spinney, I am welcomed by a combination of hardly discernible hill or dale, but of gentle fold which mere words cannot capture. The field opposite has its array of mowed methodical regimented stripes, the hay cut, a sight not dissimilar to a painting by Paul Nash. The wood is of spruce, a touch of splendour rather than splendid but considering what it is—merely spruce—it is pleasing to the eye. And the woodland floor is, surprisingly, not dark and lifeless but is covered by brambles and as far as the eye can see. Unloved spruce teaming up with equally unloved brambles to produce a rich and moving combination, supplemented by the coppiced surrounds spasmodically dotted along the woodland edge—a reminder of an earlier cultivation out on the field's edge. A partridge takes to the wing—always an unexpected clattering, unnerving performance as I hadn't seen him and he could so easily have stayed put in safety instead of a flutter and an inelegant landing in an adjacent corner at the far end of the field.

Out beyond the lane, near the now non-existent house and lake, there are rooks. They are always here, flying in noisy gatherings, breaking away, reforming, landing, peeling, ascending, silent—then the noise resumes—as they have been doing no doubt at this spot for decades, maybe centuries, that intelligent, myth associated, unappreciated companion of farm and stead, a defining gem of the open countryside, merging of man's labours and nature's works, combining all.

By step and dip and furrow
The country tells its tale
A little part of England
Green mantled by its vale.

Mind you the general vista is one of a parched and tired terrain, more so than normal even for late July—clearly a hosepipe ban in Heaven. And before returning I ate my first blackberry of the season—earlier than usual and of poor quality.

The path back is a squeezed and reluctant one—official but left to fend for itself by a farmer who wants to discourage the likes of me and maximise his crop yield. But good husbandry and conservation, commercial gain and respect for nature is an argument surely won seasons ago, for to honour one is to enhance both.

This farmer thinks otherwise. I saw him—I heard him first—bang, bang, thud, thud as I turned for home, crossing the penultimate field which on the outward journey had been home to a herd of cows, contentedly slumbering in the distant corner with two bullocks plodding gainfully towards them. On re-entering the same field, not an animal to be seen! When I reached the spot where the bangs and thuds emanated, there they were huddled awkwardly in a dark, branch covered corner and close to the tractor which, with its weight attached, was banging a fencing post into the baked earth. There was no food available—my first thought in this dry spell with the need to supplement the paucity of the diet on hand, but the cows had long since realised that the tractor hadn't brought food yet they stayed and rested the best they could beside those bangs and thuds.

***

Crossing the golf course and making a detour to the Palladium bridge, over which Queen Victoria passed to meet her Melbourne and where nearby the besotted Lady Caroline Lamb burnt her Byron love letters, I was met by the sight of pollarded willows, stark, unnatural, but given a short back and sides which will extend their lives and help them grow more quickly, but it will be a season or two before they adorn the lakeside again.

On Brocket bridge my thoughts combine.

***

We have a lovely mature ash tree in the field opposite our gate, lucky to have such a specimen but almost unlucky when a once near neighbour, no lover of nature, claimed randomly that it was dying and should be removed forthwith. A convenient prognosis by him because he thought the branches might fall across his drive. That was over 30 years ago and as I write it stands proudly in all its glory, healthy and spectacular.

Without the ash, the sheep would roam
Without the hurdle gate no home
In foregone days, the harrow, plough and spade
By ash were made.

Another fine specimen, this time of an oak, stands equally proudly in the fold of the field, at least that one was never challenged by the said neighbour.

> *Stand, stand the oak at dawn*
> *It grows in equal number*
> *To the years of its decline.*
> *Unnoticed near the lawn*
> *The early purple orchid*
> *And the open celandine.*

There are other specimen trees which act as reference points, familiar, anchored sights in an ever-changing landscape. I worry for my beech, large, old, pivotal to the orientation of the garden but it has a shallow root formation and no doubt is especially vulnerable in these regularly dry summers. But so far so good. Generally, I detect that some of the ancient trees on the walks are somewhat distressed and could benefit from a few trees in their proximity being removed thereby offering them the space they need, and giving us the opportunity to enjoy them to the full and for more generations to come.

And then there are the two trees, a pair which are a little party piece, the signature trees of Capability Brown, small in his time, almost mere bushes but now fully grown specimens. They creaked, they bent, they almost fell down in a storm but they seem to have made a full recovery and are splendid in their bold statement that Mr. Brown worked here.

But I return to my oak in the fold, probably no more than 250 years old. I hope it makes twice that age and touches the second half of the present millennium.

> *The sturdy oak, its growth conveys*
> *The summers past of countless days.*

There is nothing particularly special about a 250-year-old oak, many places possess at least one, but I can see mine every day, merely by glancing up or when I draw back the curtains on a new day. That is special! Last night, a full moon cast its silver rays through the landing skylight; I turned back the curtains. The lawn, the field, my oak, my ash were all visible in their silvery hue. It was 4 a.m. and paradise.

Another oak, the sessile, is even closer to my desk, a mere 100 feet away. It supplies the giraffes at the local zoo with fodder, one of their favourite treats. I know that because the tree surgeon tells me that he takes my cuttings to them.

***

I have noticed recently, in this dry spell, that the nettles which usually rapidly colonise my bug pile—an ecological gesture for the little creatures which help the bigger ones to survive, are thin on the ground. Is it because of the dry weather— or more sinister—has the devil left that part of the garden—the Devil's Plaything—and gone a visiting elsewhere?

There is a loveliness that settles on this hour
When fading nettles join the yearly round
And robin red by autumn takes its turn
With martin, swift and swallow on the wing
And bending bowers where thrushes sing.

Each morning, I am welcomed by the one remaining white dove, always accompanied by its mate, a wood pigeon, the two are inseparable. Noah, I call the dove. The latter is a free loader but I try to appreciate it, easier when the sun illuminates its feathers, the blue and greys, violet and green. I am beginning to like it—but why do I never get a jackdaw despite there being plenty around, even on the nearby roundabout; nor collar doves—which are rare now, but I have the appropriate habitat and I enrich it with such birds in mind. Not fair.

* * *

Today I walked through a modern squeezer gate, well I think that is what it's supposed to be, which has been installed recently. Unlike its traditional relative, made of wood and even—rarely—of stone—and wondrously on occasion made of two upright stones with gentle curves, this one is metal and it looks hideous and always will do. I know of a few who could never get through it; they would reach that spot and see the glories beyond but, like Moses, only see and be denied access to the Promised Land.

The first person I meet in the "Promised Land" is an elderly lady with two dogs. 'One is deaf and the other is disobedient,' she says and walks on.

Adjacent to this squeezer gate grows one of my least favourite plants, the silverweed. My dislike is illogical and even embarrassing but harbouring such dislikes, fortunately is rare, at least until I get older. I am not sure either why the harmless silverweed—they were once eaten—should fall into that category. In a way it is rather special with its silver pale matt effect which produces a scene change in the wind. In fact, I am beginning to like it!

* * *

An advantage of living in a supposedly crowded island but with wide open views and dotted with countless hamlets, is the ready sight of a church tower, or spire or spike depending on the part of the country, with variations, and in different materials, such as a round tower or square one, to add to the ancient mix. Today I heard the clock strike. The chime of passing time yet it is in itself timeless, a dichotomy to ponder as I walk through the shaded tunnel between two high banks, perhaps a drover's way.

The harvest safely home
And I to tea
By the fading wood
And aged yew, a special tree

Below a passing sky
I know not where
Drover's way or lane
Will lead, by ancient track, nor care.

My luck is in, the Shetland ponies are friendly; usually they either ignore me or appear, on occasion, aggressive, typical of a smaller version of many living things. The ponies nuzzle and insist upon more affection. To each of us equal joy but I move on before they tell me that they are sated. I don't want their version of that's enough.

When I turn left down the lime tree avenue, I stop on this perfect day to look across the fields to the distant town, such a far prospect; without the binoculars, easy to ignore or be aware of. What do all those buildings signify—those offices with their routines, hierarches, deadlines, careers, meetings about meetings—and the shops where instant gratification is on hand at different prices? For me, right now, I have a deeper joy and it is free. I know it is deeper. There is no presumption as I have experienced both, and often, and, despite everyone being different, the open air, the feel and sound of nature, beats the lot—and it is both free and always available.

***

Once I was asked where I had wandered that day and when I told them they asked where that was, despite being locals themselves. 'Where it has always been,' I said boldly. That didn't endear me but to me it was a worthy riposte to the interminable recollections of foreign holidays past and of plans of those to come; predictable chat with the diluted caveat that one day, perhaps, they will discover their own country and the little corners on their very doorstep. I could have given a fuller answer;

By nature's brush with fetching hue
The bluebells paint the woodland blue
The sudden sound of pheasant cocks
The rhythm of the morning fox
With stealth will mark the melting dew.

Where brambles climb and oaks preside
Once drover's way, now woodland ride
The leaning ash with hollow lea
A jumbled puzzle of a tree
Stands guard to nettles by its side.

Dull skylark gives the sweetest song
Sound of heaven than earth belong
With age the hedgerow takes its name
And choicest show of fare to claim
Where feasting eyes should linger long.

There are two gates on this walk, both standard, weathered and wooden and neither has any rhyme or reason for being plonked where they are. They block a clearly delineated route with no way of making a detour to avoid them. Yet there they are to be opened, shut and accommodated. There is even a utilitarian metal gate for the disabled, for them a hazard not a help. I have no idea how much it cost me and others. One nearby, so not on this walk, has a path around the gate itself, made by frustrated walkers so there stands that gate in non-splendid isolation, a folly and a statement, looking incongruous and purposeless.

Ah, but there is a silence settling on the view, no sound of human activity, nor of the constant activity of nature as it goes about its daily routines. It is a great wonder how nature has the ability, via wind, to turn on or off, up or down, the volume of a road, often far away. There is also silence by nature where there would be noise by man to undertake a comparable task. Take the oak in the near field, in the middle, isolated by the plough but a lone oak and a fine one. It would be pumping gallons of water constantly to its every branch right up to the canopy, an achievement which, via humans, would require a large and very noisy mechanical pump. Pretty clever. If it were beside me, I would give it a hug.

I wonder whether George Bernard Shaw got his idea for some of his plays whilst walking this very walk—*Pygmalion* perhaps and thus *My Fair Lady; St Joan* and thus the English tide in France is turned?

It is so special today that I wouldn't give him much credit if he had been inspired by a similar day when nature combines to put on one of its finest acts. Mrs Alexander went up a hill beside my beloved Dunster one afternoon over a hundred summers ago, and wrote the hymn, *All Things Bright and Beautiful,* dead simple—and in that case, knowing that hill, a done deal in any weather.

***

I know the temperature, at least the minimum it must be, because of the profusion of butterflies. They will not appear if the temperature is below 17°. I can also tell which month we are in from the hop growing around the front of the house; it joins above the dining room windows in late July, early August, and I have a sun dial. I have everything in this digital age. I could live as a hermit. I must scan the advertisements to see if there are any jobs vacant as there were in bygone eras.

* * *

I like the contrast when in a big city and surrounded by the many, to ponder the tranquillity of this rural retreat. To contrast the constant movement with nature's constant yet calming endeavours. I looked back across the old, old meadow to the Palladium church, then the other way to the distant folds, a ploughed sloping field framing the fields beyond, defined by hedgerow and woods—and the sky allowing a small intense patch of sunlight to highlight one field but then a minute later, the sky changes, the view changes and the field no longer highlighted.

Full leaf and flower, the cream of summer days.

An experience, based on a view, unique, transitory and now gone forever. I turn to proceed along the path, crushing a berry.

A fallen leaf
A token of the passing year
Near perfect, yet so brief
And soon to disappear.

A jewel unbound
Yet hanging long to be enjoyed
A berry crushed upon the ground
A work of art destroyed.

I cut across the field of corn, fair-waved the golden corn, to the big house and cut back on myself to make a short cut avoiding later the need to climb the lane, a long steady incline which today, in the heat, would constitute a steep hill. As I re-emerge onto the green way, I pass a jogger, clearly struggling. I like to give a cheery, bouncy greeting and await an acknowledgement from an often-exhausted stranger. A touch of unwelcome ragwort adds a splash of yellow to the fading pink of the common mallow and to the paler, minted clusters of the water mint beside the fast-flowing river. Up the lane, as it ascends from the lowest point at the ford, both sides are strewn with a thin even layer of hay, discarded by a trailer but adding an unfamiliar twist to a familiar sight, whilst on the road, in places, are squashed berries, and at the ridge top, a big pink rose hangs heavily over the estate cottage garden boundary as if to view the scene beyond with a white buddleia for company.

I was thinking as I meandered, how random life can be. Each step will crush an array of inserts that happen to be in my path at that moment, on a spot of my choosing, when I could have stepped elsewhere. I then began to think of the sheep and cows, currently chewing the cud contentedly, and realised that some of them, somewhere, will be partly eaten by me. Two living things. One to be sacrificed for the other.

On my return, I gave my boots a thorough cleaning and reflected that over the previous year I must have walked the equivalent of from here to Rome. My walks were, indeed are, in a way, a kind of pilgrimage, a celebration. I reflected also that I am basically a creature of circumstance, usually walking the walks the same way round, hardly ever doing a clockwise one anti-clockwise or vice versa—but when I do, the walk has a totally different feel to it. Strange.

***

I notice today that the field margins close to the big house have been cut. Fine for the time of year to ensure no doubt that the insects fall into the undergrowth and the soil does not benefit from the nutrients of the cut itself. But here the exercise looked manicured, a tidying up exercise to accommodate a view from a garden.

The landscape is liberally dotted with smaller manor houses tucked away to be discovered in the dip of the lane, often added to, now matured, merging into the original, rather like the renovations—saving in many cases—of old manor houses in the 1890s until the outbreak of war in 1939. But these local examples often suffer from being too orderly even taking into account their recent treatment and considering how they will look in time when also weathered. One near the Palladium church has plantings near the gate which are best left in a private estate of bespoke executive homes, and the gates are ostentatious whilst the field beside the garden is mowed with plantings and little spinneys, and with netting to keep out deer and rabbits. The whole doesn't add up.

On the turn back to the village green, there is a pile of branches. I was there three seasons ago when the large branch fell, unannounced, and duly blocked the path soon to be hacked and piled into a copious heap beside the way. Now, a mere few years later, that pile is low, the overall area it covers considerably reduced. The wonder, the silent efficient wonder, of nature. Evidence of a God!

***

As I meander freely across the countryside, not as freely as did dear tormented Clare before the enclosures, a privilege still available even today in its limited form, and one which not many can enjoy in other countries without our crucial right to roam, I celebrate nature whilst lamenting the declining biodiversity; I make a detour to a corner of a field which this year hasn't been ploughed, a small rectangular patch. I am richly rewarded.

I tell the truth!
The butterfly upon the thistle flower
Soon not one but many
And the moment soon an hour.

If the unmatched Richard Jefferies walked the Pilgrims Way today as he once did just over a century ago, I doubt that he would note the same rich array of fauna and flora. My little untouched set aside, confined to meagre margins, perhaps is comparable to what Jefferies saw throughout his long walk and may now even exceed it. Here we have bindweed, lesser celandine, wild-oats, oxeye daises and a few stray and stranded bluebells—a reminder that the woodland had a greater cover—sweet cicely and dog's mercury—and a few more no doubt if I knew my wild flowers a little better.

Their mist of fragrance binding.

On occasion we have a one-off, unannounced display such as a carpeted hillside of foxgloves where the woodland has been cleared.

Foxgloves not by invitation gained yet stay as friend
In garden, dell and ditch and hollow by the stream
Till nearly summer's end.

We also have an apple tree in the hedgerow, the result of a discarded apple core—or, on rarer occasions, deliberately planted reflecting a practice of bygone days. And then there is the gorse, present on one walk and in one spot only. I often wonder why a species doesn't colonise further as it must have replaced another originally. This gorse too might indicate that the area was once different, hinting of a former rough open space.

I feel sorry for some other species; take the snowdrop. It pops up, adorns the banks, the old rampart between church and castle at a nearby village, draws its hosts of admirers, then disappears before the delights of spring and is fast asleep throughout the summer and other seasons.

Ah but the winter has its moment, equal but not for all, a different script for winter days.

The year has turned, the ragwort heads the queue
The lower wood with snowdrops covered now
And strutting in the morning dew
The rook returns.

The lane back from the green way is designated a "Quiet Lane" but a cautious driver needs to hoot their horn at each and every bend making the spot one of the nosiest.

* * *

Up on the Icknield Way, at the start of the walk which I sometimes do and where the Romans walked and where once now long forgotten farm labourers toiled, is a village where George Orwell lived and probably based Animal Farm. I gaze at the empty farmyard, at the farmer's house and at the track from the yard and look around, unsuccessfully, for the windmill. What pleases me most and gladdens my heart is that this little configuration of modest buildings was the very likely bait which infuriated the Soviet Kremlin. It had its moment and has now slipped contentedly and quietly into its English rural idyll and solitude—job done.

Places do that, a stately home that was once the abode of a family which owned great wealth and enjoyed the great power which usually accompanied it; the stone grave in a corner of a village church which is the last resting place of a Chief Secretary who served his monarch, with his wife's grave adjacent—the "property of the above"—who now languishes in a mortal's tomb, equal in eternity, dust to dust, often eventually forgotten.

* * *

I was a little perplexed on my walk today, off the green way and before the path takes me across the wide open field where once we walked our beloved pigmy goats—Gaston and Spencer—'Come on, Gaston, come on, Spencer,'—I look round but they are no longer there—there is a large grassy patch which is never ploughed. This morning a very large area had been flattened—as if oversized lovers were there before me or an unidentified animal had rollicked and rolled in abandon.

I have passed this spot many times. Once there were two lovers enjoying themselves as young lovers should and I often wonder what became of their love, requited then, cold now—or on every tree is mistletoe!

Before the white of elderflower
Becomes the nip of autumn fair
Between the sway of summer yield
On hedge and down, on fell and field
On lake and shore, on fen and heath
Lovers kiss and vow.

In summer breeze, the roses nod their heads
And lovers vow their dreams.

Being still very hot, I cut back onto the lane rather than proceed to the field's end where in winter the corner is waterlogged and in summer the crops struggle to survive.

From south the wind blew lightly
And I by westward home.

I notice that the intrusive Japanese knotweed which grew in the bank beside the house which once belonged to the railway company which in turn ran this now defunct line, its style of architecture as deliberate and distinctive as if it were a cottage on a rural estate, has been eradicated. No doubt at last.

***

There is a walk I do when visiting my daughter and her family which takes in the last easterly outcrop of the Chilterns, affording fine views of the flat Cambridgeshire countryside with both Cambridge and Ely in sight but the range begins—or ends—in Oxfordshire almost in sight of Oxford's dreamy spires. No wonder it didn't take long to burn the beacons on the string of hills and warn England of a pending threat.

On the left as I descend the tree lined lane which runs parallel to a minor road with breaks in the hedging to afford glimpses of those distant prospects and where grows it seems every locally found wildflower except tansy, their colours mixing as on an artist's pallet, there is a track and rail, the several, for the training of racehorses. One was Oxo, the winner of the 1959 Grand National and I remember that day despite being so young and so long ago. I ask where he was buried. Nobody knows nor cares. Probably as feed to other animals. Poor Oxo.

My walks vary in their detail, much due to the terrain of hill and dale, of river and exposed escarpment, of soil and the touch of man, embellished by the weather.

The wind will pipe the seasons on
What music dance the swallow high?

We are assuredly blessed therefore to have the distinctive changing seasons, deprived of that gear change only rarely, unlike the experience of less happier lands.

Just as we are blessed by being never more than about 70 miles from the sea, hence having more salt in the soil, more worms to eat, dictating a more liberal and expansive lifestyle for some species such as the badger which can spread out rather than concentrate in one location. An academic point no doubt if the man from the ministry comes to gas you.

But there are other elements which touch the scene, paint the rural portrait and add to its delights. We don't have large rivers in these parts but we do have rivers—chalk streams to boot, so significant, and the moving water, the bending or broken branches, the shallows, the eddies of a miniature shoreline, the weir, the little rocks, the high water levels in winter and the lower ones in summer, the fast flow and the quiet steady timeless movement, all are there for me and for others to enjoy. Here on hot days in July the blue dragonflies will entertain, their colour a sublime magnificence.

A branch falls and a new habitat is created, changed, adjusted, matures as the seasons pass. The purple loosestrife with its long spikes waves at me, from its watery domain as I pass.

The water at the ford at the turn of a walk has flowed over the road only occasionally in 30 years, skimming the road surface, a delight to watch, to walk through, to rest against the rail and to watch the waters form, out of view, contemplate their journey, through fields, woods, beside nettles, thistles and docks, the plants of neglected places, then joining the bigger river further down, which, in turn, joins with another, to combine and reach as one the big river before flowing finally to the sea.

By the rushes by the waters
The placid heron stands
Whilst nestled quietly in the lee
Beside the oldest apple tree
In tangled glade
And dappled shade
Is where the blackbird sings

It all combines to become the fragile construct of our idyllic countryside.

And over all the skylark sings.

But then again other factors join the mix to determine the nature of a walk, not just the seasons, the weather, the soil. A sound can change the mood of a walk, of a scene. In late spring, if lucky, the cuckoo is heard far away, beside the distant woodland, getting up to no good but with a finesse, a dexterity which defies criticism, not a view , however, held by the meadow pippit or by the dunnock, the nests of choice of this enigmatic, opportunistic bird.

The waving wheat and barley
And cuckoo's first heard song.

Then on my return, the wren awaits me. The wren, often heard, seldom seen.

The wrens at dawn are singing
Sweet tones, sharp notes, and trills.

Sobering, levelling that two political giants of a former age, Lord Grey, the Foreign Secretary when the lights went out at the commencement of the Great War, and former President Theodore Roosevelt, would study this little feathered fellow, our second smallest bird and the only bird our two countries share, as retired friends in rural Hampshire.

***

With the end of the long hot spell and the reassurance that my recent comparative lethargy was not evidence of declining years but merely of the rising mercury, I am out and about again. Today the walk takes me past the Queen Anne house, with its display of brickwork, tall chimneys and pinnacles, peeping across the fields and almost beckoning me to come closer. A peculiar walk; for years I did it without realising that a small section was the same piece but repeated and reached when one loop joins another. The vast vistas, everything, seemed different but was the same, merely reached from another angle and after a long interval and detour.

As I reach the Queen Anne house, I peep through the fencing to glimpse cheekily but with admiration at the garden of this noble pile, what lingering memories afforded for those whose blessed childhoods were spent here, looking out at dawn over the beckoning fields and verdant ways, of endless childhood and long hot English summer days. Near this house is a busy livery with two horses, full size to scale, made entirely of old horseshoes, one rearing, the other placid, guarding the entrance to the yard.

***

Today the sloes adorn the hedges. Their colour defies definition, so I will not attempt it. Suffice to say the berries in the sun by the wayside were as beguiling as they could possibly be. Before them, deep in the field edge, is a cluster of Lords and Ladies, bright red, lamp like, excelling surely in the intricacy of their making rather than in the beauty of their depiction.

The final two fields at the end of the walk, one cut but not ploughed, the other already ploughed, are divided by the footpath.

Two stages of the farmer's cycle, side by side and I reflect on the field still to be tilled, recalling the previous late summer when the birds in their numbers followed the plough, gulls in particular and in their hundreds.

***

I wish I had my binoculars today with the swallows diving and darting as only they can do along with the swifts and the house martins. Last year a little later and to my left where the telegraph poles march, they were congregating in profusion awaiting the instinctive call of nature to fly, fly away, beyond the most distant horizon, hopefully to return to this same sacred little spot next year.

The wide-open vista of patchwork fields and gentle undulation is a piece of heaven here on earth. (How is it that so often we have spinney, hill, field, fold and view just where it should be?) I stop rooted to the spot, as anchored as the woodland at my side. Last winter about here, I passed two walkers. They wore heavy protective gear, both assisted by two adjustable sticks, yet the temperature was 9° and we were not that far from the nearest tube station! They looked like two yetis. We engaged briefly as I had passed them earlier. They said at least I had the wind behind me returning but it was uphill too and they wondered which was the most challenging, a climb or the wind.

It is, in so many ways, unreal, unbelievable even in its modest beauty. Astronauts eulogise about the beauty of the bubble earth as viewed from space; no need to venture up when merely a glance across these fields would convince any jury.

And what they don't describe because they are not up in space long enough or cannot compare the same view in two different seasons, is how the view can be snow covered, blessed with sun, battered by winds, deluged by rains—and remain supreme.

Nor can they hear from their position of disadvantage, the birdsong that echoes in and around the woods or the owl in the stillness of the night.

***

Does nature make those who are fellow wanderers placid and kindly or does nature merely attract those sorts? I do not know but I have my thoughts. Oh, sweet natured Clare, that dear demented tortured laureate of the countryside, who wandered far until enclosed by a changing idyll. He, above all, could engage and be at one with nature, the go-between. "I hunted curious flowers in rapture and muttered thoughts in their praise."

***

I am full of thoughts today as I pass the ruined church and enter the field which once was threatened by needless greedy developers but fortunately sense and sentiment prevailed and so I enter a meadow and not attempt to avoid a mini housing estate. Once here many years ago we erected a maypole with an American friend who adopted and absorbed all things English during his brief stay, and even a Scottish touch come Burns Night. He has long since returned to the States and another there that day is long since dead.

But I do meet two couples from America on the steps of the church—they admire all things bright and beautiful hereabouts and invite me to their restaurant in "Old Boston."

Across the next field, wide, broad, almost Capability Brown in its layout to the gate beside the new plantation—I say "new" but it must be over 20 years since it was planted, taking a corner of a field and transforming it into a traditional managed woodland with high grasses, wildflowers, biodiversity in a single gesture, a worthy legacy. Further on another plantation, also recent, smaller but quite lacking in logic and aesthetics, a piece of planting which makes an unsophisticated statement.

A few days earlier when I was passing this spot, a lamb came over from the middle of the field, curious, fearless, and friendly. I patted it and roughed it behind its ears. What a little fellow, but, no doubt, soon to meet his preordained, inevitable destiny. Last year in the "Capability Brown" field the lambs played and made up games along and over the bank, beside the hanging boarder trees, making it their playground. Later that year all were penned awaiting transfer and soon the field was silent. Happy brief time, growing up but never grown up—and now we have this year's lambs replacing them and the cycle starts again. There are a few poppies hereabouts.

* * *

Today's walk over a stone bridge where once I was menaced by cows, threatened by signs, entertained by boxing hares, is still one of my favourites, but this time approached from a different angle, avoiding these hazards. Today there are people about wading in the river, others on the bank, some taking notes and yet more liaising importantly in the field. I ask what is going on; they tell me they are seeking a film location. The bridge once appeared in a TV series and I recognised it instantly. Whether the river was chosen this time around I do not know but not to my knowledge. At least it vindicates my conclusion that these relatively unknown parts are special, or is it merely that they are only seven miles from London and therefore there is no need to incur the cost of overnight accommodation?

At the top of the field—and what a peculiar field, mown wide pathways almost like rides and the rest always left to grass, never cut and the same applies to the fields beyond the ridge, is a rather ugly large house made more so by a utilitarian concrete drive, possibly Second World War in origin; it has that feel about it. Nor can I get excited by the woods hereabouts although once, when I passed the lodge and turned left down the lane when rain was heavy, the lane resembled a fast-flowing stream and the sunshine added a magical touch. For once, I didn't have my camera. I finished the walk in a sprint and returned to capture the view.

I am reminded of these woods in a different season when the snowdrops adorn the lanes and carpet the woodland floor. Then they are at their best.

Beguiled by snowdrops in the winter light.

But today as I pass the house to reach these other fields where the grass grows but is never cut, I watch the dogs taking their owners for a walk and the activity in the livery for the ponies.

In pastures green and plenty.

***

The skylarks are in full throttle, the lane traces the higher ground and the distant sound of cricket being played—I know that field but cannot as yet see it from here—only the church spire is in view, but cricket and church, skylark and peacetime. Those who fought in the trenches might have fought for this vision and personification of Englishness and wondered if such a combination would ever return. Well it did, largely thanks to their sacrifice but they in their numbers, alas, never did.

Today the wind is stronger here than usual, yet the skylarks—the ones I can see—are steady on the wing, hovering miracles watching over their nests. They worry when I pass because their nests are on the ground nearby. I tell them not to be concerned but they mistake me for another.

Above the clouds are performing. Strange that their names never caught on, to become common parlour, unlike that of plants. Oh, to look up and to say 'ah a lamb's wool sky' or 'I see a mare's tail'. I could lie in a field and watch the clouds on days like these. It helps somehow if the spot is higher than the surroundings, even if only by a little, but great whenever or whatever.

The distant lane defines the field
As clouds above the sky.

I pass the houses on the green, their names depict their origins—The Old Post House to name but one. But they are more than that to me as I ponder each one without hopefully appearing nosey. At last Remembrance Sunday, after useful research by one parishioner, we were able to put a person to the name on our war memorial and a home to a name—a cobbler, a lowly labourer, a blacksmith, or, more often, their sons, leaving one day, closing the garden gate, crossing the green, giving a wave, a probable final goodbye.

***

As I walked today with the autumn mists blanketing the familiar outline of field and hedge, but in so doing announcing autumn's lease is ending, I tried to recall how some great writers on nature described a view or a piece of wildlife.

Birdsong fades as summer turns.

In truth, I started reflecting before the walk with the sound of the resident blackbird. Richard Jefferies wrote, "blackbird, in whose throat the sweetness of the green fields dwell," how beautiful and true, and he continued with his "the sunbeams—sank deeper and deeper into the wheat ears."

One of my favourites, the now largely forgotten Walter Murray, could write "I caught an occasional glimpse of the intricate and complex pattern of life, and once or twice, as fleeting as the rainbow- flash from a trembling dewdrop, I perceived that all these things were but the external signs of a kingdom such as I had never dreamed of; that the colours were as a drop- curtain which, while it might never rise to disclose the stage within, grew transparent before my wondering eyes." Nearly 100 summers have passed since then.

In more recent times, H E Bates, referring to a wood local when a boy wrote, "the smell of them was tranquilising, the old soft sweetness of wood—earth, mustily sweet, the immemorial distilling of uncountable flowers and leaves, the odour that only comes from the timeless decay under trees in almost sunless places, the black scent of ceaseless growing and dying and fermentation." He didn't notice the smell until "autumn, at the damp turn of the year."

The leaves are golden, yellow now
Or pink or purple, float to ground
Till gusty winds ascend anew
And let me see again the view.
Cherries once red by berry, now by leaf
Others still bright red or dusty brown
October has arrived.

Or Laurie Lee on the peculiar splendour of an English spring, "longer here, lingering voluptuously over the passive landscape, like the trembling wing of some drowsy bird stretched in a trance and loath to leave it…Spring in England is a prolonged adolescence, stumbling, sweet and slow, a thing of infinitesimal shades, false starts, expectations, deferred hopes and final showers of glory." Wow.

Such writings also make me sad, sad for the loss of birdsong and of habitats, gone in many places, perhaps forever and with their loss the absence of words once familiar now excluded even from dictionaries and diction.

"And if the fullest frenzy of song, with nightingales and blackbirds mad in the drowsy hay-noon's of June, has not been reached, there is a clarity and a shouting of bird life everywhere that is like a silver mocking of winter." H E Bates again, and like A E Housman it doesn't matter much if it makes complete sense or not, it is the order of words and their choice which unlocks our emotions. How often today that combination of birdsong, the deep enriching of emotions, inculcated, stirred, teased by nature, is on offer? Hopefully on hold rather than consigned to memories of a near forgotten past. So recent in the story of things overall—but so far away.

Before embarking on my walk today, I noticed the welcome return of the nuthatch, a favourite of mine despite its rather jerky manner, dull colours, unusual shape made more so by the black streak along the head and its rather cheeky fluffy bottom. Always alone, never as a pair. It is the king of my nut holder. Tits in profusion, both blue and great make a hasty deferential exit on its arrival. Across the lawn the magpie competes with the squirrel for the nuts—and wins, 1-0 each to the nuthatch and to the magpie in a small version of the great game of survival. Recently, I even saw a magpie chase a squirrel across the lawn.

I cross the lane which once was part of the busy road to London, with only its cat's eyes as a reminder. It is a quiet backwater now. Where once lorries thundered and I travelled as a child, expectations high, for London and the Christmas lights, it is a lane in all but name.

Now I, the man, cross it in order to enter the path down into the wood and beyond. The path, recently also resurfaced, is already shaded by long, dangling, rather tired growth of the fading summer.

The summer lease is ending
The season's mottled hue
The squirrel's larder filling
A winter's moon in view.

Further on, the lane cuts down and through a small wood plantation with high earth banks on each side.

Shadows deep in valleys fair.

Why is such a simple combination so beguiling and not only when the sun's rays touch the surface, passing through the branches like a silent symphony from the pen of a musical maestro.

On my return, the thrush has made an appearance, the first time in many years. My lucky day. Once so common, now so rare in these parts at least. Will I see pied wagtail and cap my day and complete the regular visitors to the lawn of my childhood? Not on this occasion, alas.

When I write these notes, with my cat on my lap, it is dark outside and the mistle thrush sings.

At the season's end I seek the old familiar places of the earlier days of spring and summer. I am not depressed. I walk the heavy earth alone, few venture forth at this time of year on days like these. There is a pigeon struggling, pushing on its breast, moving slowly and awkwardly, seeking the relative camouflage of the path's edge. I should, I know, dispatch it rather than leave it to the fox, but I cannot. On my return, it has made its journey's end, wedged into the deepest thicket, still alive, but awaiting death with patience and resignation.

I pass the place where swallows in the late summer awaited the instinctive call to depart. Empty and silent now. There is a distinct autumnal freshness pervading the clear crisp air. I reflect on many walks and seasons and I am deeply content.

The sap no longer rises
And I no longer roam
So take my hand, but gently
And make the ground my home.